WIZOO Quick Start

Reinhard Schmitz

MIDI

Imprint

Author   Reinhard Schmitz
Publisher   Peter Gorges

Cover art   design box, Ravensburg, Germany
Interior design and layout   Uwe Senkler

Order No.   WZ 00722
International Standard Book Number   0-8256-1909-2

Exclusive Distributors:
Music Sales Corporation
257 Park Avenue South, New York, NY 10010 USA

Music Sales Limited
8/9 Frith Street, London W1D 3JB England

Music Sales Pty. Limited
120 Rothschild Street, Rosebery, Sydney, NSW 2018, Australia

Printed in the United States of America
by Vicks Lithograph and Printing Corporation

Welcome

Like all Wizoo Quick Start guides, this book is here to help you understand the topic as swiftly and painlessly as possible. This is why the Quick Start guides are written in a clear, easy-to-understand language. And with the included CD-ROM, you'll have plenty of opportunities to gain hands-on experience.

In today's world, anyone who wants to make music using electronic instruments or computers is faced with understanding MIDI. But what exactly is MIDI? How does it work? We can't see or hear it, so the answers to these questions are anything but obvious.

This book provides the answers, and by the time you've finished reading you'll know exactly what MIDI is. And even if you don't have any prior musical training or technical knowledge, by investing a few hours reading this book, you too can enjoy the untold possibilities that exist in the world of MIDI.

So here's wishing you hours of fun reading and experimenting, and lots of success playing music via MIDI.

Peter Gorges, Publisher

Table of Contents

1 What Is MIDI?   7

How Does an Instrument Work?   7
How Does a MIDI Instrument Work?   9
What Does the Word "MIDI" Mean?   11
What MIDI Can and Can't Do   12
What Is a MIDI Sequencer?   14

2 MIDI in Practice   18

In, Out, and Thru—the MIDI Ports   18
How to Turn Your Computer into a MIDI Device   19
How to Connect Your MIDI System   21
What Is a MIDI Channel?   26
One Instrument, Many Sounds—Multitimbral Versus Polyphonic   27
How to Make Music with MIDI   30

3 What Are MIDI Files?   39

4 What Is General MIDI?   41

5 Frequently Asked Questions   44

6 Troubleshooting   45

7 Internet Links   47

8 CD-ROM Contents   48

What Is MIDI?

"MIDI is the language that electronic musical instruments use to talk to each other," was the best answer I could come up with at short notice when my son's yen for knowledge turned to music at the tender age of six and he asked me, "What is this MIDI stuff?" At my reply he nodded and came back with, "So this box makes a sound when I press a button on this box." That description of MIDI pretty much sums it up for me to this day.

However, the boy had the advantage of having watched his father at work on many occasions, and since I haven't had the pleasure of your company in my studio, you'll be treated to a more detailed explanation in this book. Warming up to the subject gradually, let's leave electronics behind for the moment and turn to the world of conventional instruments.

How Does an Instrument Work?

Even if you don't play an instrument, chances are you've seen a musician playing an instrument at concerts or on TV. So what does a musician do to call forth sounds from an instrument?

Case in point: A pianist presses a key on the keyboard of a grand or upright piano, and the instrument sounds a note.

The same principle holds true for other instruments: The musician performs a specific action—like plucking a string or blowing air into a mouthpiece—and the given instrument sounds a note. Say we wanted to define the shortest possible formula for the action (the musician presses a key) and reaction (a note sounds) involved in playing an instrument. Since the musician's action is telling the instrument what to do, we could call this process a *note on* command.

When a piano player presses a key on the piano, a note sounds. We'll call this a *note on* command.

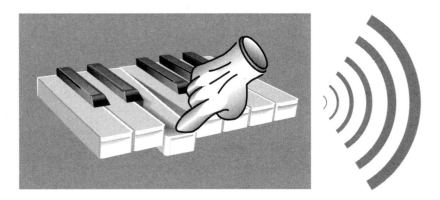

Now let's look at how a musician silences a note. Turning again to the first example, when our trusty pianist releases the key he's pressing, the note stops sounding. Here too the musician performs an action (he releases the key) that causes a specific response (the note stops sounding). Again, the musician's action is telling the instrument what to do, so we'll call this process a *note off* command.

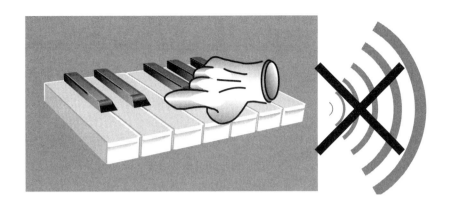

When a pianist releases a key on the piano, the note he was playing stops sounding. We'll describe this as a *note off* command.

Basically, that's all you need to know to understand how an instrument works.

How Does a MIDI Instrument Work?

In principle, a MIDI instrument works just like a conventional instrument. Take, for example, a MIDI instrument with keys, which in the world of electronic musical instruments is called a *MIDI keyboard*. When musicians go to play notes, they simply press a key just like the pianist would on the piano. Same action, same reaction, same designation—a *note on* command.

Though the process of activating a note is the same, the way in which the sound is generated is markedly different. When a key on a piano is pressed, a mechanism inside the piano is activated, causing a hammer to strike a string. The sound we hear is generated by the vibrating string.

Pressing a key on a MIDI keyboard turns on a switch, which is connected to a microprocessor, which is a chip capable of detecting that this switch is now *on*. The microprocessor relays this information to the keyboard's sound generator, prompting it to generate a note.

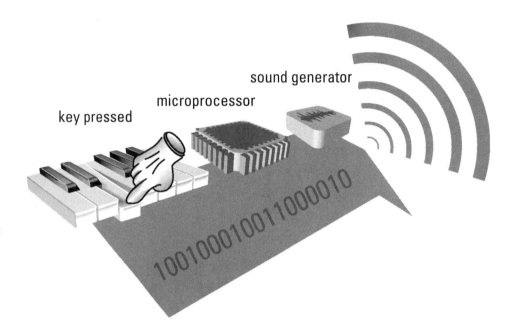

Just like on a piano, a note sounds when a key is pressed on a MIDI keyboard. Again, we'll call this process a *note on* command.

The method may be different, but the outcome is the same, so this process can also be described as a *note on* command. And by the way, you've just encountered your first MIDI command. When a key on a MIDI keyboard is pressed, the microprocessor translates this information into a *note on* command before sending it to the sound generator.

You can probably predict what happens when the key on a MIDI keyboard is released. The microprocessor detects that the key, which serves as a switch, is set to *off*. It translates this information into a command and forwards the message to the sound generator. The sound generator stops producing the note at this command and, in MIDI language, the message is called a *note off* command. So now you know two MIDI commands.

What Does the Word "MIDI" Mean?

MIDI is an acronym for *Musical Instrument Digital Interface*.

Although this monster of a technical term is certainly a mouthful, there's no reason to be intimidated by it. I can assure you that lurking behind this wordy facade is a very simple meaning. So let's break it down and take a closer look at the various terms.

We'll examine the word *digital* first. It tells you that MIDI information is stored and processed in the form of numbers. For instance, say you press a key on a MIDI keyboard. This event is translated into numbers (there's our *note on* command again), which are to MIDI devices what the alphabet, words, and sentences are to us. They tell everyone with a need to know that a note is being played and which note that is. But more on this a little later.

The word *interface* suggests that data may be exchanged among several devices. If you own a PC, you may be aware that your computer sends data to your printer via a parallel or USB interface. MIDI does the same with musical information, except that it's sent to another MIDI device (rather than a printer) for processing.

Two connected words remain, *musical instrument*. Since these are pretty self-explanatory, I won't waste your time by defining them—but allow me to make an observation. Strictly speaking, *musical instrument* doesn't get to the heart of the matter because, although MIDI commands can be triggered by acoustic instruments, the sound generator is always an *electronic* musical instrument.

If I was asked to condense the meaning of the words making up the acronym "MIDI" in a simple and straightforward statement, I'd simply repeat the opening sentence of this book: "MIDI is the language that electronic music instruments use to talk to each other."

"Great," I can imagine you thinking, "but what's in it for me?" Good question—the following section explains all about what MIDI can do for you.

What MIDI Can and Can't Do

MIDI makes it possible to connect together several stand-alone devices and instruments to create a system.

A MIDI set-up lets you:

A *sequencer* is a hardware device or software application for recording and playing back MIDI information.

❖ play several electronic instruments using the same keyboard,

❖ record the music you play on your instrument to a *sequencer* (see page 14) and have it play back the recorded music,

❖ *synchronize* all types of recording devices—both MIDI sequencers and conventional audio recorders—so they're locked in step with each other, and

❖ record the movements of control features on mixers and signal processors, and have the system carry out their actions automatically.

This list of MIDI capabilities is far from complete, but it does give you a first impression of what MIDI can do for you.

At first glance, the capabilities of MIDI seem boundless.
This has been known to inspire a few misconceptions:

❖ MIDI is used to connect several devices together. This
means that a lone MIDI device's MIDI functions are,
for all practical purposes, dormant. You must connect
it to one or several other MIDI devices to awaken these
MIDI functions.

❖ MIDI doesn't transmit audio signals. Say you own two
keyboards and you want to hear the sounds of both
instruments. Connecting them via a MIDI circuit
won't get the job done. To be able to hear them both,
you must connect the audio outputs of the two instruments to your monitoring system.

❖ Different instruments can't swap sounds via MIDI.
Case in point: Say you connected a sound generator by
manufacturer X to a sound generator by manufacturer
Y via MIDI. One of the sound generators features an
awesome strings "patch"—in music-speak, a synthetic
sound or instrument—that you want to transfer to the
other sound generator. As convenient as that could be,
it's just not possible. Every manufacturer uses a sound
generator of his own design, which always differs
from the designs of other manufacturers, and, in
many cases, even the sound generators of different
models by the *same* manufacturer differ. This also
holds true for other devices such as effectors and signal processors.

What Is a MIDI Sequencer?

Although a sweeping survey of all the many different types of MIDI devices is beyond the scope of this book, allow me an exception with the MIDI *sequencer.* There are two good reasons for us to take a closer look at this mysterious beast: For one, a MIDI sequencer is the ideal nerve center of a MIDI system, and for the other, it best illustrates the benefits that MIDI brings to the musician.

MIDI sequencers record and play back MIDI information and are available in the form of dedicated hardware devices, built-in functional sections on keyboards, and software for computers. Today, this last-mentioned guise is the most widespread, with its popularity owing to remarkable ease of use and an abundance of features. You'll find out how to transform your computer into a MIDI device starting on page 19.

In the interests of understanding how very convenient a MIDI sequencer can be, let's first look at what takes place in a conventional audio recording scenario. Say you own a keyboard and a recording device of some type, perhaps a cassette or MD recorder. You want to record a song you like to play on your keyboard, so you connect the audio output of your keyboard to the audio input of your recording setup. You arm the recorder, press the record button, capture your performance, and your song is *in the can,* as audio engineers like to say. What if you make a mistake, though? Right, back you go, re-arm the recorder, and record everything again. What if something again goes wrong during the second pass? If at first you don't succeed, try again. And again, and again, ad nauseam ...

This situation is very different when you record your song using a MIDI sequencer because it doesn't record the actual music, it simply registers which keys you played (you will recall our discussion of the *note on* command) and when you played them. If you tell the sequencer to play back the passage you recorded, it sends this information concerning what you played to the sound generator of your keyboard, which plays your song back exactly the way you played it.

Here's what makes MIDI so convenient: MIDI recordings have a tremendous advantage over audio recordings because the sequencer stores the notes you play as data. Not only can you view this data in the sequencer, you can actually edit it at will. If you make a mistake, all you have to do is pinpoint the bum notes and fix them.

And you don't have to be a programmer to do this. All sequencers display musical information in views that are easily understood, either in the form of a plain text list, as musical notes, or in some type of graphical representation. Usually you get a selection of different views and are free to chose the one you prefer to work with.

The following illustration shows a common display type called a "grid" or "piano roll" where the notes you play are represented as bars. These bars are arrayed on a grid arranged in musical measures and the pitches of the individual notes are shown on the keyboard pictured on the left.

This is what the notes you play look like in the *grid* or *piano roll* view of a MIDI sequencer. Each of the bars represents a note. You can shift the bars as desired to edit the respective notes. That makes fixing mistakes a piece of cake.

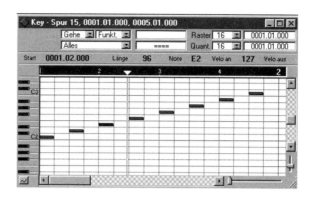

If you want to change a note, simply grab the bar representing that note and drag it to the desired position. Now that's far easier than re-recording the entire song, wouldn't you agree?

I hope this little example succeeded in illustrating the advantages of recording music using a MIDI sequencer, particularly over recording audio using traditional methods. If it didn't, I hedged a few arguments that are sure to convince you.

At the mere touch of a button, MIDI sequencers let you:

❖ transpose a composition or parts thereof,

❖ change the tempo of a song,

❖ shift notes that missed their mark to the right bar position automatically (in the MIDI vernacular this is called *quantizing*),

❖ replace the sound of the instrument that you used to record a passage with the sound of another instrument, such as choosing a guitar patch for the melody you originally recorded with a piano patch,

❖ copy any parts of a song to any desired position, which spares you the trouble of recording challenging passages several times. Simply nail that part once, and copy it as often as you like.

In a nutshell, a MIDI sequencer grants you total control over a music production, and for this reason, it's an unrivalled recording tool.

If this section whet your appetite for working with a MIDI sequencer, you're in luck: On the included CD-ROM, you'll find a demo version of Steinberg's *Cubase VST* MIDI sequencer. Why not install this package on your computer and take it for a spin ...

However, before you dive right in the wonderful world of sequencing, I recommend that you at least read the following chapter first. It describes how you can configure individual MIDI instruments and MIDI devices to set up a MIDI system, and you'll also learn about the most important MIDI commands.

MIDI in Practice 2

In, Out, and Thru—the MIDI Ports

The connectors required to link a bunch of stand-alone MIDI devices to create a MIDI system are usually located on the rear panels of the devices. These are implemented in the form of 5-pin DIN ports.

The MIDI specification calls for at least one "MIDI In" and one "MIDI Out" port, but on many devices you will also find a third connector, the "MIDI Thru" port. These connectors look something like this:

In, Out, and Thru—the MIDI ports

The MIDI ports may look identical, but each serves a different purpose and the labels on the ports tell you what that purpose is:

❖ MIDI In receives MIDI data sent from another MIDI device.

❖ MIDI Out sends MIDI data generated by the device to other devices. To enable another device to receive and process this data, the MIDI Out of the sending device must be connected to the MIDI In of the receiving device.

❖ MIDI Thru forwards an exact copy of data received via the MIDI In port to another device. You'll learn more about the practical benefits of the MIDI Thru port in the section "How to Connect Your MIDI System" on page 21.

> MIDI Thru doesn't send MIDI data generated by the device. Only the MIDI Out port can do that.

How to Turn Your Computer into a MIDI Device

If you own a computer, you already have a very powerful and extremely versatile MIDI device at your disposal.

With a suitable software program, your computer can play virtually every role in a MIDI system. It can play the part of a MIDI sequencer (see page 14) or of several MIDI sound generators. And equipped with the right software, state-of-the-art personal computers may even be transformed into fully-blown music studios incorporating all conceivable MIDI devices and audio recording, processing, and playback options.

However, your computer probably lacks an important feature—a communication channel. For our purposes, it can't do without an interface to the outside MIDI world.

Let's assume you want to use your computer as a MIDI sequencer. You play the notes you want to record on a musical keyboard (you know, the one with the ebony and ivory keys). But where do you connect your keyboard? Your computer doesn't offer MIDI ports.

You can solve this problem by connecting a MIDI interface, which enables you to connect your computer to other MIDI devices.

It takes a MIDI interface to turn your computer into a real MIDI device.

MIDI interfaces come in a variety of guises and sport price tags that vary from dirt cheap to budget-busting; however, the benchmark feature is always the number of MIDI inputs and outputs. Basic bargain-bin models offer one MIDI In and one MIDI Out, and as the number of ins and outs rises, so does the number on the price tag. Without knowing your goals and requirements, I can't tell you which MIDI interface is best for you. I suggest that you talk to the folks at a reputable music store.

With any luck, your computer may already be equipped with a hidden MIDI interface as the joystick port on many soundcards is also capable of sending and receiving MIDI commands. You can plug a special adapter equipped with a MIDI In and MIDI Out connector to the joystick port, and if this special adapter doesn't ship with your soundcard, you shouldn't have any trouble locating one at your local music, computer, or electronics store.

How to Connect Your MIDI System

You'll require special cables to connect your MIDI devices together, and MIDI cables sport 5-pin DIN connectors on both ends. The connectors are provided with a ridge that fits snuggly into a matching notch on the devices' MIDI ports, and the idea is to make sure we plug the connector into the port properly. Unfortunately, manufacturers were unable to agree on a standard layout, particularly concerning the orientation of the ports, so the process of cabling up MIDI devices often degenerates into an exercise in patience. Don't despair, though, the pros have to contend with the same "poke and hope" problems.

MIDI cords come in a variety of lengths, and the maximum allowable length, according to the MIDI specification, is 15 meters. The reasons for this are of a technical nature and need not concern us further, though there's one thing well worth remembering: Always use the shortest cords possible.

Now that we know about MIDI ports and cables, we can take a closer look at how to go about connecting MIDI devices to set up a system. Let's begin with a simple scenario illustrating exactly what MIDI is all about, and for purposes of an example, let's say we want to play two or more instruments using the same keyboard.

To do this, you must connect the MIDI Out of the instrument whose keyboard you want to use for control purposes, to the MIDI In of the instrument that you want to control. This creates a simple MIDI system consisting of a *master* (the controlling instrument, A) and a *slave* (the controlled instrument, B).

In a MIDI system, a device that sends data to other devices is called the *master*, while devices that receive data are called *slaves*.

21

A simple MIDI system: Instrument A as well as instrument B can be played using the keyboard of instrument A.

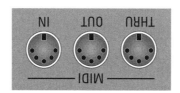

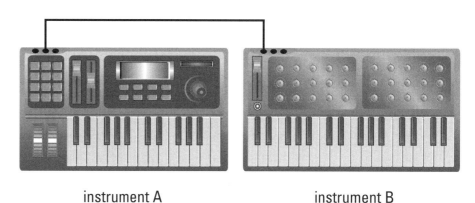

instrument A   instrument B

Now, say you want to use each keyboard to control the other instrument. No problem: Connect the MIDI Out of the instrument that was the slave (B) in the previous example, to the MIDI In of the instrument that was the master (A). Now the slave can also be the master and vice-versa. In other words, each of the two instruments can send *and* receive MIDI data.

Say we want to connect three or more MIDI devices. This is where the MIDI Thru port enters the picture. You will recall that the MIDI Thru sends out an exact copy of the data received via MIDI In. It could also be said that data routed to the MIDI In is simply forwarded through the device, hence the term *Thru*.

Here's a simple example:

You have three instruments at hand, and you want make instrument A the master, and instruments B and C the slaves. To achieve this configuration, simply connect instrument A's MIDI Out to instrument B's MIDI In, and then instrument B's MIDI Thru to instrument C's MIDI In. Presto—there you have your one-master, two-slaves setup. Both slaves (B and C) can be played using the keyboard on the master (A) device.

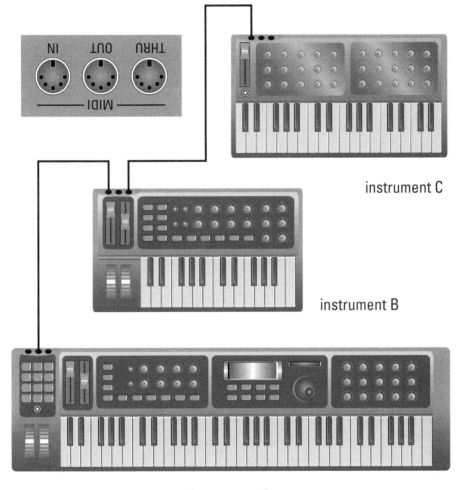

A slightly more sophisticated MIDI system: Data generated by instrument A is sent to instrument B and, at the same time, to instrument C via instrument B's MIDI Thru.

instrument C

instrument B

instrument A

In a system like the one pictured above, it's not possible to address and access instrument C using instrument B. When you play instrument B, this note data is routed to its MIDI Out rather than its MIDI Thru port, and in this setup the MIDI Out is not connected to instrument C's MIDI In.

Forwarding MIDI data with the MIDI Thru port is not a problem if a MIDI system consists of just one master and two or three slaves. In larger systems, problems may arise due to the technical limitations of MIDI, and at worst, MIDI devices located towards the end of the signal chain will no longer be able to recognize MIDI data correctly—kind of like a game of Chinese whispers!

The simplest and cheapest option for solving this problem is a "MIDI Thru box."

Be sure to use a MIDI Thru box to connect complex MIDI systems comprising of more than three slaves.

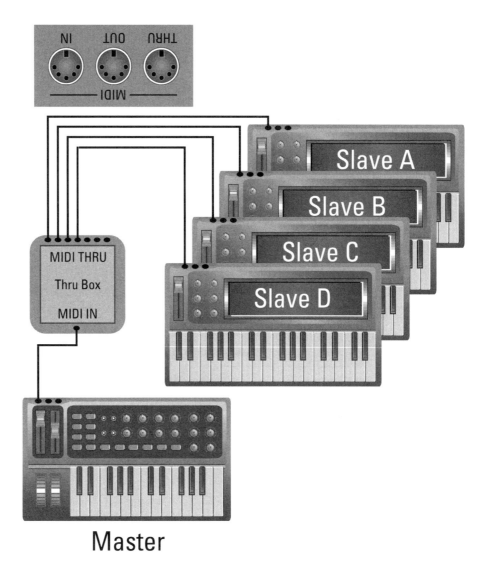

Master

A MIDI Thru box offers one MIDI In and several MIDI Thru ports—in most cases, four, eight, or sixteen. Incoming data arriving at the MIDI In port is copied to all of the MIDI Thru ports, and the circuitry of the Thru box is designed to ensure that an exact copy of the data arriving at the MIDI In is forwarded to all Thru ports simultaneously. With this solution, cabling a system couldn't be any easier: Simply connect the master's MIDI Out to the Thru box's MIDI In, and then connect each of your slaves to a MIDI Thru port of the Thru box—behold, a stable, reliable MIDI system.

> Many MIDI Thru boxes feature not one but several MIDI Ins. However, they can't be used simultaneously, so you must employ a switch to determine which MIDI In transmits data to the MIDI Thru ports.

Problems can arise if you ever need to mix MIDI data, so let's look at an example. Say you own two MIDI keyboards and want to use them simultaneously and record their data to a sequencer, but the sequencer offers just one MIDI In.

There are tales of some more adventurous home recordists who have attempted to use a simple adapter cable of the same variety used to merge audio signals, but don't make the same mistake! This solution won't work with MIDI data and destroys the data structure so that no MIDI device will be able to interpret the mess that's left.

To do this properly, you'll need a gadget called a "MIDI merge box" that offers at least two MIDI Ins and one MIDI Out. The data sent in via the two Ins is routed out via the MIDI Out. A circuit within the box merges the data arriving at both MIDI Ins according to a specific logical sequence that other MIDI devices are able to interpret accurately.

What Is a MIDI Channel?

Let's back up a bit and call to mind the example using the simplest possible MIDI system (see page 22). We have two instruments, A and B, and we want to play both devices using the keyboard of instrument A. To that end, we connect the MIDI Out of instrument A to the MIDI In of instrument B, and now when we play on instrument A, instrument B should also generate sounds.

The chances are that in this scenario, instrument B will maintain a stubborn silence despite the fact the MIDI ports and audio connectors are connected properly. The reason for this is that instrument A and B are using different MIDI *channels*.

The MIDI standard calls for key-related information and many other types of data to be accompanied by information on the channel over which this data is sent. There are a total of 16 MIDI channels available, meaning that you can address up to 16 devices independently of one another, each via a dedicated MIDI channel.

To allow the sender and receiver in a MIDI system to communicate, the sender's MIDI send channel and the receiver's MIDI receive channel must be the same.

A device where the receiving channel is set to "1" will only handle data provided with the channel designator "1." Data arriving on other channels is ignored.

On virtually all MIDI devices, you can set the channel on which MIDI data is received (the receive channel) and the channel on which MIDI data is sent (the send channel) independently of one another. How this is done varies from device to device, and if you are in any doubt, please consult your device's manual.

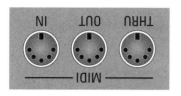

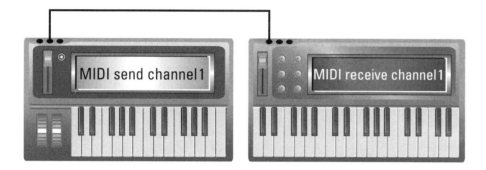

To enable MIDI devices to communicate with each other, the MIDI send channel of the sender and the MIDI receive channel of the receiver must correspond.

One Instrument, Many Sounds— Multitimbral Versus Polyphonic

In the early days of MIDI, the vast majority of sound generators were only able to send and receive data on one MIDI channel, respectively, and they were largely unable to generate several sounds simultaneously either. This meant that if you composed a song requiring several patches—for instance, piano, bass and drums—on a MIDI sequencer, playing all those instruments back was an expensive proposition: Each patch required a dedicated sound generator.

Most sound generators today are *multitimbral*. A multitimbral sound generator can produce several different sounds simultaneously, and each of these sounds may be accessed via a dedicated MIDI channel. This makes it possible to play back far more sophisticated arrangements composed of many different patches using a single sound generator.

How many sounds can be produced simultaneously and addressed separately via MIDI depends on the model of sound generator. If the manufacturer states that the device is 16-part multitimbral, this tells you that the device can generate 16 different sounds at the same time, and that they can be controlled separately via MIDI.

A multitimbral sound generator is able to produce several sounds simultaneously. Each sound may be accessed via a dedicated MIDI channel.

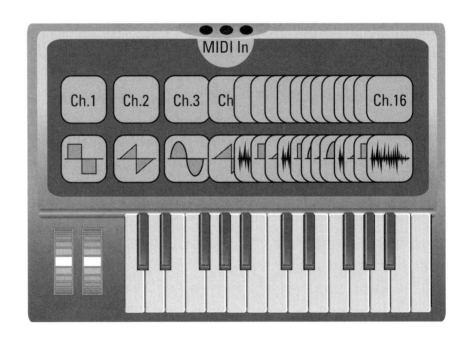

Common to most neophyte electronic musicians and home recordists is a tendency to confuse the terms *multitimbral* and *polyphony*. Though, as you will soon find out, these terms are indeed related, their meanings are completely different. *X-part multitimbral* means that the sound generator is able to produce x amount of different sounds simultaneously. In contrast, *X-voice polyphony* means that the sound generator is able to play no more than x amount of notes simultaneously.

The following example should clarify the connection between the two. Say your sound generator offers 16-voice polyphony and 16-part multitimbral capability. This means you can access 16 sounds at the same time via MIDI. However, from a statistical perspective, you only have one voice available for each sound. In theory, it's not possible to use one sound for several different notes—in other words, you can't play a chord.

In practice, things are not quite so bleak as manufacturers came up with two ways to mitigate this problem. For one, modern sound generators do not assign voices *statically* as in the above example using a fixed voice-to-sound assignment. Instead, they assign voices *dynamically*. Dynamic voice assignment means the available voices are assigned to sounds on demand, which sounds complicated, but is really very simple. Let's look at an example.

Imagine a sequencer that addresses three sounds of a 16-voice sound generator, a bass, a piano and a strings patch. In the course of the song, the bass requires two, the piano six, and the string section ten voices in total. If the voice assignments were static or fixed, we would be two voices short of a song.

In contrast, a device that assigns voices dynamically, constantly monitors sounds to check how many voices they require at any given place in the song. The voices are then assigned according to demand, meaning that if the arrangement never uses more than 16 voices at the same time, your song will be played back without any problems.

Manufacturers are taking another approach to resolving the great "multitimbral versus polyphony" issue, and that is to release ever more affordable sound generators with a mind-boggling number of voices. Today, devices with 64 or even 128 voices are not uncommon.

How to Make Music with MIDI

Before we rush headlong into this section, allow me to refresh your memory and recap the general definition of MIDI as we formulated it at the beginning of this book: "MIDI is the language that electronic music instruments use to talk to each other."

In this context, the term *message* describes an individual word of the MIDI language.

So MIDI is a language, and like every language, MIDI uses words. A word in the MIDI language is called a *message*. The following section will familiarize you with the most important messages you'll come across when playing music via MIDI.

Playing Sounds via MIDI

You encountered the most important and most frequently used MIDI message at the beginning of this book, the "note on" message (see the section "How Does a MIDI Instrument Work?" on page 9). Accordingly, a note on message means "switch note on" or, on a MIDI keyboard, "press key."

If you picture a keyboard on a MIDI instrument, you will agree that the command "press key" leaves a lot of room for interpretation. You may ask, "How does the generator know which key was pressed, which note was switched on?" And if you have ever watched a keyboardist's fingers at work, you may be curious to know "How hard was the key pressed, how loud is the note that was switched on?" All these questions are entirely justified, and the note on message has the answers.

When you press a key, the keyboard registers more than the change in status from *off* to *on*. This action generates three types of information, indicating:

❖ that a key was pressed,

❖ which key was pressed, and

❖ how hard the key was pressed.

That first statement is called a "status byte." It is identical for every key because it merely indicates that a key was pressed.

The second statement is called the "first data byte." It varies according to which key was played. MIDI recognizes keys from C-2 to G8 and simply numbers these from bottom to top. The number of a key is called the "MIDI note number." Feel free to count them if you please, but I assure you that there are exactly 128 note numbers from C-2 to G8. And that's more than enough, considering a concert grand has a range of only 88 keys.

To help you achieve a deeper understanding of the relationship between keys and their note numbers, let's examine the layout of a musical keyboard.

You can see that, starting from the "C" key and moving in ascending order, every key is a half-step higher than the preceding key. The pattern repeats after 12 keys, though, with notes an octave higher.

On a musical keyboard, of
the type found on a piano,
keys are designated by let-
ters of the alphabet rather
than by numbers.

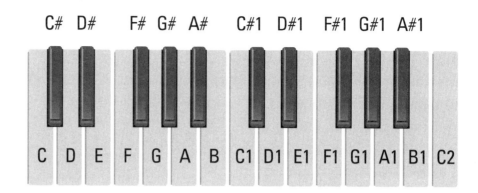

The following illustration shows the relationship between MIDI note numbers and the 88 keys on the keyboard of a piano. Note the "C" assigned to the note
number 60. This note is also known as the "middle C,"
as its position lies at the middle of the piano keyboard.
However, this key is not necessarily located at the middle
of a MIDI keyboard. Even if it's located at a position other
than the center of the keyboard, the key with the note
value of "middle C" may still be called the "middle C."

The relationship between
the range of a piano key-
board and the MIDI note
numbers. "Middle C" is
defined as note number 60.

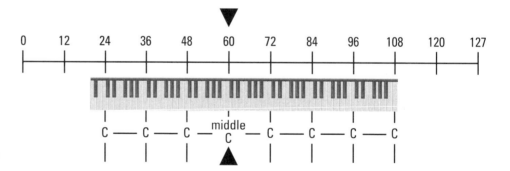

That brings us to the third bit of information relayed in a
note on message, the "second data byte." This value varies according to how hard you press the key, though this
explanation is somewhat misleading. In physical terms,
the measure here is the speed of travel, rather than the
amount of pressure. More pressure means the key covers

the distance from top to bottom faster, which is why this information is called "velocity" in MIDI-speak. Velocity data is usually used to determine the volume of a note within a range of 1 (very soft) to 127 (peak level).

> To be able to generate velocity data, a keyboard must satisfy certain technical prerequisites. Specifically, it must be able to gauge your attack (that's the amount of pressure your touch exerts, which determines the key's speed of travel) dynamically. Touch-sensitive keyboards have sensors that measure the time it takes a key to travel from top to bottom.

Now you know what happens when you press a key. But what takes place when you release it? Cutting right to the chase, a "note off" message is generated containing the information that a key was released, which key was released, and how fast the key was released. As soon as a sound generator receives a note off command, it stops playing the sound.

Often a note on message with a velocity value of 0 is used instead of a note off message. Different approach, same effect.

Selecting Sounds via MIDI

Another important type of MIDI command is the "program change" message, which is used to activate another program within a MIDI device, such as a patch in a MIDI sound generator, via remote control. Program change messages have a value range of 0 to 127, which means they may be used to address up to 128 sound programs.

There are a couple of pitfalls that you should be aware of when you're dealing with program change messages. For one, the sounds of different devices are almost always assigned to different program numbers. An example: On synthesizer A, a piano patch is stored in program number 5, and on synthesizer B, program number 5 holds a strings patch. If synthesizer A sends a program change

Note that a program change message doesn't send a patch to the receiver. It simply tells the device to activate another patch.

message to synthesizer B for program 5, you will hear strings rather than a piano.

Another potential headache is the different ways in which devices' memories are organized. On some devices, these programs (or memory slots) start with 0, while others begin with 1. So if you want to select a patch on the latter device via a MIDI message sent from the former device, you must send a program change with a value of 49 to select program 50. That's easy math, but it gets tougher if the manufacturer decided to order the programs according to an "octonary" system (which means in groups of 8) so that group 1 is made up of programs 11 to 18, group 2 of programs 21 to 28, and so on.

Despite carrying out a seemingly simple task, program change commands rank among the most useful of all MIDI commands. Say you composed a ballad in a sequencer, arranging it so that a piano plays accompaniment during the verses and, in the chorus, a strings patch takes over. You can of course access different sound generators via different MIDI channels and let them play these two patches. However, the more convenient and certainly less expensive solution is to send a program change command every time a chorus follows a verse (and vice versa) so that the sound generator switches back and forth between the piano and the strings patches. That spares you the cost of a second sound generator or, if you already own another synth, lets you use it for other applications.

A tip on developing good MIDI habits: Don't send program change messages to a sound generator while it's busy processing note information. Always send program changes during "breaks," and give the sound generator a moment to process a program change message before you start feeding notes to it again.

Changing Sounds via MIDI

Please refer to the illustration below when you're reading the following section as it should help you gain a better understanding of this topic.

The wheels, knobs, switches, and pedals depicted in the picture are all used to change sounds in some way while you're playing. For instance, when you move the pitch-bend wheel, it generates instructions that tell the instrument to change the pitch of the note. In the following section, I'll introduce you to some of the most important control commands and discuss their effects on sounds.

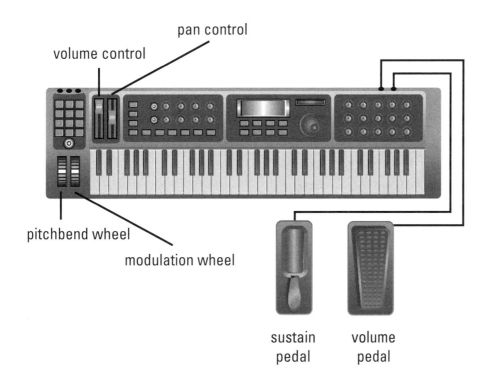

pan control

volume control

pitchbend wheel

modulation wheel

sustain pedal

volume pedal

Electronic keyboard instruments bristle with wheels, knobs, switches, and pedals. These control features let you modify sounds on the fly while you are playing.

Pitchbend Wheel

The pitchbend wheel varies the pitch of a note smoothly, meaning in infinitely variable increments rather than in audible steps. This effect is great for imitating the sound of a guitar string being bent, slide guitar, pedal steel, and the like.

Pitchbend wheels normally have a center detent, which is often spring-loaded so that the wheel automatically returns to the center position when released. The pitch remains unchanged at the center position and turning the pitchbend wheel upwards from the center position or away from you raises the note, downwards or towards you lowers the note.

As you may have already guessed, the MIDI message generated by a pitchbend wheel is called a "pitchbend change." It has a value range of 0 to 127, whereby 64 indicates the center position. Values lower than 64 cause the note's pitch to drop, higher values raise it.

> Note that you must define to which extent the pitch is changed by the action of the pitchbend wheel on the receiving rather than the sending device. Consult the manual of your sound generator to learn how and where to do this.

Modulation Wheel

Vibrato is a periodic alternation of pitch, where as *tremolo* is a periodic change of volume.

As its name would suggest, the modulation wheel is used to *modulate* a sound. In practice, the modulation wheel is commonly used to create effects called *vibrato* and *tremolo*.

The MIDI messages generated by a modulation wheel belong to a group of messages called "control change" commands, or simply "controllers." There are a total of

120 controllers and every controller has a number. This number enables the receiver to identify the controller and assign it to a specific function. The modulation wheel is controller number 1.

When you turn the modulation wheel from its lowest possible position to its highest, it generates continuously increasing values from 0 (bottom position, no modulation) to 127 (top position, maximum modulation).

Volume Pedal

A volume pedal, slider, or knob is used to vary the level, and the MIDI message responsible for volume control is controller 7 ("channel volume"). Controller 7 also has a value range of 0 to 127, whereby 0 elicits total silence and 127 the loudest possible volume or peak level.

Pan Control

Controller 10 ("pan") determines the panorama setting, which is the sound's position in the stereo spread. Controller 10 can have a value range of 0 to 127, whereby 64 indicates the center position. At that position, the sound is spread in equal parts over the two stereo channels. The value 0 indicates the far left position, and value 127 the far right.

Sustain Pedal

A sustain or hold pedal enables notes to continue to sound after keys have been released. They carry on sounding until the pedal is released.

The MIDI message used to do this is controller 64 ("damper pedal, sustain") and in one respect, this controller is quite different from the controllers discussed so far.

While these controllers in some way *modulate* something, say a change in volume from very soft to very loud, controller 64 is simply a switch. There are just two statuses—the pedal is either pressed or released. Accordingly, controller 64 requires just two values. The MIDI language calls for the receiver to interpret values of 0 to 63 as "off" (pedal up) and values of 64 to 127 as "on" (pedal floored).

What Are MIDI Files?

MIDI files were devised to allow songs to be exchanged among different sequencers. Since nearly every model of sequencer stores data in its own format, a song created on sequencer model A can't be played back on sequencer model B and vice versa.

The official name for MIDI files is "Standard MIDI Files," or "SMF" for short.

If you store the song as a MIDI file, every sequencer under the sun that supports this standard can play it.

MIDI files come in three formats: 0, 1, and 2, though only the first two are of interest to us:

❖ Format 0 merges all MIDI tracks of a song into a single track. It is primarily suited for use with simple MIDI players that are able to handle just one track.

❖ Format 1 keeps the information on the individual tracks of a song separate; and even the track names remain intact. This format is the best choice when you want to swap songs among multitrack sequencers.

Creating MIDI files on a sequencer that supports this standard is easily done. All you have to do is select the *Save as MIDI file* option, which, on a software sequencer, is usually found in the File menu. And during the save process, you're often given a choice of saving the MIDI file in format 0 or 1 (see above).

What Are MIDI Files?

Next to commercial MIDI files, there are lots of files available free of charge. You'll find the addresses of some good Internet sources on page 47.

Today there's a glut of commercial MIDI files available, and you can get practically every hit by artists ranging from Elvis to Madonna, as well as a vast repertoire of classical pieces. Of course, you may opt to simply play these MIDI files, but that's rather pointless. Far more fun is the nifty option of muting certain instrument tracks in your sequencer so you can play those parts—say melodies or bass lines—yourself while the rest of the instruments accompany you. Try doing that with a CD!

> I compiled a couple of MIDI files for you in the folder "MIDI Files," which you'll find on the CD that accompanies this book. Please feel free to experiment with them.

One of the major drawbacks of MIDI files is that they contain no information on the sounds employed in the composition. If you record a MIDI file using one type of sound generator and at some point play it back over another sound generator, expect to hear something completely different from what you composed. You can solve that problem by selecting sounds according to the "General MIDI specification," and then playing the song on a General MIDI sound generator, which neatly brings us to the next chapter where you'll find out what General MIDI is all about.

What Is General MIDI?

4

"General MIDI," or "GM" for short, is a standard for sound generators that defines specific sounds and specific MIDI program number assignments for these sounds. As a result, a MIDI song created on a General MIDI sound generator will sound largely the same when you play it back on another General MIDI sound generator.

Among other stuff, the GM standard defines the following minimum specifications for a GM sound generator:

❖ 24-voice polyphonic sound generator with dynamic voice administration,

❖ 16-part multitimbral capability; in other words, MIDI data reception on all 16 MIDI channels, whereby a different sound may be addressed over every channel; channel 10 is reserved for drum and percussion sounds,

❖ 128 sound programs in 16 categories or *families* in accordance with the specifications of the "GM Sound Set" (see below). And, in addition, 47 drum and percussion sounds in accordance with the specifications of the "GM Percussion Map" (see below).

Here's the GM Sound Set:

The number that comes before the name of a sound stands for the MIDI program change number by which the sound may be selected.

#		#		#		#	
1	Acoustic Grand Piano	33	Acoustic Bass	65	Soprano Sax	97	Fx 1 (rain)
2	Bright Acoustic Piano	34	Electric Bass (finger)	66	Alto Sax	98	Fx 2 (soundtrack)
3	Electric Grand Piano	35	Electric Bass (pick)	67	Tenor Sax	99	Fx 3 (crystal)
4	Honky-tonk Piano	36	Fretless Bass	68	Baritone Sax	100	Fx 4 (atmosphere)
5	Electric Piano 1	37	Slap Bass 1	69	Oboe	101	Fx 5 (brightness)
6	Electric Piano 2	38	Slap Bass 2	70	English Horn	102	Fx 6 (goblins)
7	Harpsichord	39	Synth Bass 1	71	Bassoon	103	Fx 7 (echoes)
8	Clavi	40	Synth Bass 2	72	Clarinet	104	Fx 8 (sci-fi)
9	Celesta	41	Violin	73	Piccolo	105	Sitar
10	Glockenspiel	42	Viola	74	Flute	106	Banjo
11	Music Box	43	Cello	75	Recorder	107	Shamisen
12	Vibraphone	44	Contrabass	76	Pan Flute	108	Koto
13	Marimba	45	Tremolo Strings	77	Blown Bottle	109	Kalimba
14	Xylophone	46	Pizzicato Strings	78	Shakuhachi	110	Bag pipe
15	Tubular Bells	47	Orchestral Harp	79	Whistle	111	Fiddle
16	Dulcimer	48	Timpani	80	Ocarina	112	Shanai
17	Drawbar Organ	49	String Ensemble 1	81	Lead 1 (square)	113	Tinkle Bell
18	Percussive Organ	50	String Ensemble 2	82	Lead 2 (sawtooth)	114	Agogo
19	Rock Organ	51	SynthStrings 1	83	Lead 3 (calliope)	115	Steel Drums
20	Church Organ	52	SynthStrings 2	84	Lead 4 (chiff)	116	Woodblock
21	Reed Organ	53	Choir Aahs	85	Lead 5 (charang)	117	Taiko Drum
22	Accordion	54	Voice Oohs	86	Lead 6 (voice)	118	Melodic Tom
23	Harmonica	55	Synth Voice	87	Lead 7 (fifths)	119	Synth Drum
24	Tango Accordion	56	Orchestra Hit	88	Lead 8 (bass + lead)	120	Reverse Cymbal
25	Acoustic Guitar (nylon)	57	Trumpet	89	Pad 1 (new age)	121	Guitar Fret Noise
26	Acoustic Guitar (steel)	58	Trombone	90	Pad 2 (warm)	122	Breath Noise
27	Electric Guitar (jazz)	59	Tuba	91	Pad 3 (polysynth)	123	Seashore
28	Electric Guitar (clean)	60	Muted Trumpet	92	Pad 4 (choir)	124	Bird Tweet
29	Electric Guitar (muted)	61	French Horn	93	Pad 5 (bowed)	125	Telephone Ring
30	Overdriven Guitar	62	Brass Section	94	Pad 6 (metallic)	126	Helicopter
31	Distortion Guitar	63	SynthBrass 1	95	Pad 7 (halo)	127	Applause
32	Guitar harmonics	64	SynthBrass 2	96	Pad 8 (sweep)	128	Gunshot

Again, the 47 drum and percussion sounds prescribed by GM are always addressed via channel 10. The defined MIDI note numbers address a certain sound each and the GM Percussion Map determines which note numbers address which sounds:

35	Acoustic Bass Drum	51	Ride Cymbal 1	67	High Agogo
36	Bass Drum 1	52	Chinese Cymbal	68	Low Agogo
37	Side Stick	53	Ride Bell	69	Cabasa
38	Acoustic Snare	54	Tambourine	70	Maracas
39	Hand Clap	55	Splash Cymbal	71	Short Whistle
40	Electric Snare	56	Cowbell	72	Long Whistle
41	Low Floor Tom	57	Crash Cymbal 2	73	Short Guiro
42	Closed Hi Hat	58	Vibraslap	74	Long Guiro
43	High Floor Tom	59	Ride Cymbal 2	75	Claves
44	Pedal Hi-Hat	60	Hi Bongo	76	Hi Wood Block
45	Low Tom	61	Low Bongo	77	Low Wood Block
46	Open Hi-Hat	62	Mute Hi Conga	78	Mute Cuica
47	Low-Mid Tom	63	Open Hi Conga	79	Open Cuica
48	Hi Mid Tom	64	Low Conga	80	Mute Triangle
49	Crash Cymbal 1	65	High Timbale	81	Open Triangle
50	High Tom	66	Low Timbale		

The number that comes before the name of a sound stands for the MIDI note number by which the sound may be triggered.

Many of the sound generators available today are GM-compatible and, next to pure GM devices, there are top-flight pro instruments that can be switched to GM mode. Most computer soundcards also organize their sounds according to the GM standard.

If an instrument or a computer soundcard sports a GM logo on the front panel or the box it comes in, this tells you that it is GM-compatible.

Some manufacturers developed standards of their own that expand the functionality of General MIDI. These enhanced standards offer a greater selection of sounds and more options for shaping sounds. Among the more popular of these GM expansions are Roland's GS standard and Yamaha's XG standard. Normally, instruments that support these standards are fully GM-compatible, meaning you can buy these instruments safe in the knowledge that you won't be left out of the GM fun.

Frequently Asked Questions 5

Do I need a keyboard to make music via MIDI?

Nope. For one, there are alternative instruments available such as MIDI guitars, MIDI wind instruments, and even MIDI percussion instruments. For the other, there are MIDI computer programs available that let you make music without *any* instrument by simply entering musical information via mouse or the computer's keyboard.

How do I connect MIDI devices to a computer?

By first plugging a MIDI interface into your computer (see also page 19).

Can MIDI also transmit audio signals?

No. Even if you have connected a sound generator via MIDI, you must still connect it to an audio system to be able to hear the sounds it generates.

Do I need special cables to connect MIDI devices?

MIDI systems that operate reliably are far more fun than unstable setups, so be sure to use MIDI cables designed and designated expressly for this purpose.

Troubleshooting 6

One of my MIDI devices doesn't respond to data sent its way.

First check the MIDI cables and make sure the MIDI Out of the sending device is connected to the MIDI In of the receiving device. Then find out if the sender's MIDI send channel matches the receiver's MIDI receive channel.

My MIDI sound generator responds to note messages but not to certain other commands such as pitchbend messages or controllers, etc.

Consult the sound generator's manual to see if it is designed to handle the type of data that's giving you problems. If so, check if the sound generator is filtering out this data. Many MIDI devices are equipped with a MIDI filter that can be activated to prevent it from receiving certain types of data, and if this is the case, change the MIDI filter settings.

When I record notes played on a MIDI keyboard to a sequencer, I hear every note twice.

You've encountered a *MIDI loop*. The sound generator receives the data for every note once from the keyboard, and again from the sequencer's MIDI Out. This problem is easily solved by setting the keyboard to "Local off" mode to sever the MIDI connection between the keyboard and the sound generator. If your keyboard doesn't offer this option, go to the sequencer and disable the MIDI Out during recording so that data is not sent to the keyboard. Almost all sequencers offer a "MIDI Thru" function that lets you do this.

MIDI files don't sound the way I recorded them when I play them back, though I use the same sound generator for recording and playback.

Many MIDI sequencers perceive and handle certain parameters such as volume or program change commands purely as play parameters. This means that these parameter values are only valid during playback, and they are not written into the actual MIDI tracks. If you generate a MIDI file, these play parameters are not saved because only the actual track data is stored with the MIDI files. Most sequencers offer an option where play parameters are written into the tracks. The whole idea of recording is to get a song to sound the way you want it to, so by all means make use of this function before you save a song as a MIDI file.

When I play a MIDI song, some notes in it seem to be missing.

At some points in the song, there may be more notes than your sound generator has voices. Check if this is the case (see also page 27).

Internet Links

7

http://www.midi.org/ Home page of the official MIDI mavens "MMA" (MIDI Manufacturers Association). Good source for information on the latest developments and trends in the MIDI world.

http://www.midi.com/ Many links to other MIDI sites as well as a section with technical information about MIDI. There is a message board on MIDI topics.

http://www.hitsquad.com/smm/ The *Shareware Music Machine* is presumably the world's largest website for music software, featuring more than 2,700 software applications for all prevailing computer operating systems. From MIDI sequencers to notation, from ear training to MP3 software, this place is a grab bag for everything the musician's heart desires.

http://www.multimidizone.co.uk/ Nearly 4,000 MIDI files by different artists as well as numerous MIDI files featuring music from movie and television soundtracks as well as computer and video games.

http://www.sciortino.net/music/ If you're searching for classical music in the form of MIDI files, this is the place for you.

CD-ROM Contents 8

Windows Software

Cubase VST Win folder   A demo version of Steinberg's Cubase VST sequencer.

MIDI Utilities Win folder   Here you'll find a collection of MIDI-related software such as MIDI file players, a MIDI input analyzer, and a handy program to transform your computer's keyboard into a "MIDI-Keyboard."

Macintosh Software

Cubase VST Mac folder   A demo version of Steinberg's Cubase VST sequencer.

MIDI Utilities Mac folder   Here you'll find a useful collection of MIDI-related tools for your Mac.

MIDI Files

This folder contains a collection of license-free MIDI files, collected for your listening pleasure! And don't forget to explore them with your sequencer's editor windows so you can see how they've been put together.

80025 75540